Breakdown of the Subsequent Convictions Associated with Criminal Aliens Placed in a Non-Custodial Setting in Fiscal Year 2013

The following table provides a breakdown of convictions associated with the 36,007 criminal aliens placed in a non-custodial setting in fiscal year 2013. The convictions occurred following release from ICE custody.

ALIEN	CONVICTION(S)
1	PETTY THEFT W/PR JAIL:SPEC OFFENSES‖ PROBATION VIOL:REARREST/REVOKE
2	NO ARREST RECEIVED‖ SEE COMMENT FOR CHARGE[1]
3	NO ARREST RECEIVED‖ THEFT
4	POSSESS CONTROL SUBSTANCE FOR SALE‖ TRANSPORT/ETC CONTROL SUBSTANCE
5	POSSESS CONTROLLED SUBSTANCE
5	POSSESS CONTROLLED SUBSTANCE
6	TAKE VEH W/O OWN CONSENT/VEH THEFT
7	TRESPASSING
8	HALLUCINOGEN-MFR
9	POSSESS NARC CONTROL SUBSTANCE
10	INFLICT CORPORAL INJ SPOUSE/COHAB
11	NO ARREST RECEIVED‖ SEE COMMENT FOR CHARGE
11	NO ARREST RECEIVED‖ VANDALISM
11	NO ARREST RECEIVED‖ SEE COMMENT FOR CHARGE
12	POSSESS CONTROLLED SUBSTANCE‖ USE/UNDER INFL CONTRLD SUBSTANCE‖ POSS ID OF 10+ PERSON W/ INT
13	RESIDENTIAL BURGLARY‖ POSSESSION OF BURGLARY TOOLS‖ KNOWINGLY DAMAGE PROPERTY
14	POSSESS NARC CONTROL SUBSTANCE
14	BURGLARY
15	LARCENY - LESS THAN $200
16	BURGLARY:SECOND DEGREE
17	POSS/PURCHASE COCAINE BASE F/SALE‖ PRCS:FLASH INCARCERATION
18	NO ARREST RECEIVED‖ CHARGE NOT SPECIFIED
19	TRANSPORT/SELL NARC/CNTL SUB
20	DISORDERLY INTOX
21	INFLICT CORPORAL INJ SPOUSE/COHAB
22	VANDALISM

ALIEN	CONVICTION(S)
23	TRANSPORT/SELL NARC/CNTL SUB
24	RECKLESS DRIVING:PARKING FACILITY
25	POSSESS CONTROLLED SUBSTANCE
26	POSSESS NARC CONTROL SUBSTANCE
	TRANSPORT/SELL NARC/CNTL SUB
27	OBSTRUCTS/RESISTS PUBLIC OFFICER/ETC
28	POSSESS NARC CONTROL SUBSTANCE
29	SPEEDING‖ DRIVING WITHOUT DRIVERS LICENSE / EXPIRED
30	VIO CS/DRUG/DEV AND COSMETIC ACT
	VIO CS/DRUG/DEV AND COSMETIC ACT
31	FORCE/ADW NOT FIREARM:GBI LIKELY
32	DISORDERLY INTOX‖ RESISTING OFFICER
33	POSS/PURCHASE COCAINE BASE F/SALE
34	TRANSPORT/SELL NARC/CNTL SUB
35	BURGLARY
36	SELL/FURNISH/ETC MARIJUANA/HASH‖ POSSESS MARIJUANA FOR SALE
37	TRANSPORT/SELL NARC/CNTL SUB
38	POSSESS CONTROLLED SUBSTANCE‖ FAIL TO APPEAR:WRITTEN PROMISE
39	POSSESS NARC CONTROL SUBSTANCE
40	POST RELEASE COMMUNITY SUPV VIOLATION
41	CRIMINAL TRESPASS
42	FALSE ID TO SPECIFIC PEACE OFICERS
43	POSSESS CONTROL SUBSTANCE FOR SALE‖ TRANSPORT/ETC CONTROL SUBSTANCE‖ VIOLATION OF PAROLE:FELONY
44	TAKE VEH W/O OWN CONSENT/VEH THEFT
45	POSSESS CONTROLLED SUBSTANCE‖ PROBATION VIOL:REARREST/REVOKE
46	FAIL COMPLY REGISTR SEX OFENDR
47	BURGLARY
48	INFLICT CORPORAL INJ ON SPOUSE/COHAB‖ VIOLATION OF PAROLE:FELONY
49	POSSESS CONTROLLED SUBSTANCE
50	ASSAULT
51	THREATEN CRIME WITH INTENT TO TERRORIZE
52	PETTY THEFT W/PR JAIL:SPEC OFFENSES
	POSSESS CONCENTRATED CANNABIS

ALIEN	CONVICTION(S)
53	VIOLATION OF PAROLE:FELONY
54	LOCAL ORDINANCE VIOLATION
55	POSSESSION CONTROLLED SUBSTANCE‖ RECEIVE KNOWN STOLEN PROPERTY
56	BURGLARY‖ RECEIVE/ETC KNOWN STOLEN PROPERTY‖ OBSTRUCT/ETC PUBLIC OFFICER/ETC
	NO ARREST RECEIVED‖ SEE COMMENT FOR CHARGE
57	BATTERY
58	TRANSPORT/ETC CONTROL SUBSTANCE
59	NONMOVING TRAFFIC VIOL
60	TRANSPORT/SELL NARC/CNTL SUB
61	GRAND THEFT:MONEY/LABOR/PROP
62	LARCENY
63	POSSESS STOLEN VEHICLE/VESSEL/ETC
64	NO ARREST RECEIVED‖ FT/REG/ETC:FEL SEX OFF/PR
65	: 13CR1726
	CONSPIRACY TO TRANSPORT ILLEGAL ALIENS‖ SRTV (TRANSPORTN OF ILLEGAL ALIEN, A/A
66	LARCENY
67	POSSESS NARC CONTROL SUBSTANCE‖ THEFT
68	POSSESS CONTROLLED SUBSTANCE‖ POSSESS UNLAW PARAPHERNALIA
69	POSS OF FIREARMS AND AMMUNITION BY AN UNLAWFUL USER OF OR PERSON ADDICTED TO A C‖ VIOLATION OF SUPERVISED RELEASE
70	GET CREDIT/ETC:USE OTHER'S ID
71	CONTEMPT:DISOBEY COURT ORDER/ETC
	BATTERY
72	POSSESS STOLEN VEHICLE/VESSEL/ETC
73	POSSESS CONTROL SUBSTANCE FOR SALE‖ POSSESS CONTROL SUBSTANCE PARAPHERNA
74	POSSESS CONTROLLED SUBSTANCE
75	VIO CRT ORD TO PREVNT DOMESTC VIOL
76	NO ARREST RECEIVED‖ SEE COMMENT FOR CHARGE
77	POST RELEASE COMMUNITY SUPV VIOLATION
	POST RELEASE COMMUNITY SUPV VIOLATION
	NO ARREST RECEIVED‖ SEE COMMENT FOR CHARGE
78	DUI:ALCOHOL/DRUGS

ALIEN	CONVICTION(S)
79	POSS MARIJUANA OVER 28.5 GRAMS|| POSSESS CONTROL SUBSTANCE PARAPHERNA|| POST RELEASE COMMUNITY SUPV VIOLATION
80	PROBATION VIOL:REARREST/REVOKE|| POSSESS/ETC BURGLARY TOOLS
81	THEFT
82	POSSESS NARC CONTROL SUBSTANCE|| USE/UNDER INFL CONTRLD SUBSTANCE
83	POSSESS CONTROLLED SUBSTANCE
84	POSSESS CONTROL SUBSTANCE FOR SALE|| OBSTRUCT/ETC PUBLIC OFFICER/ETC
	NO ARREST RECEIVED|| SEE COMMENT FOR CHARGE
	OBSTRUCT/ETC PUBLIC OFFICER/ETC
85	DUI ALCOHOL/0.08 PERCENT
86	POSSESS NARC CONTROL SUBSTANCE|| POSSESS UNLAW PARAPHERNALIA
87	NO ARREST RECEIVED|| FAIL TO APPEAR AFTER WRITTEN PROMISE
	NO ARREST RECEIVED|| FAIL TO APPEAR AFTER WRITTEN PROMISE
	NO ARREST RECEIVED|| FAIL TO APPEAR AFTER WRITTEN PROMISE
	NO ARREST RECEIVED|| FAIL TO APPEAR AFTER WRITTEN PROMISE
	TRESPAS OBSTRUC/ETC BUSINES OPR/ETC
88	FELON/ADDICT POSS/ETC FIREARM|| FALSE ID TO SPECIFIC PEACE OFICERS
89	USE/UNDER INFL CONTRLD SUBSTANCE|| POSSESS CONTROL SUBSTANCE PARAPHERNA|| DUI ALCOHOL/DRUGS|| HIT& RUN PROP DAMAG:LOC/ETC REQ|| POST RELEASE COMMUNITY SUPV VIOLATION
90	OBSTRUCT/ETC PUBLIC OFFICER/ETC
91	GRAND THEFT:AUTO|| TAKE VEH W/O OWN CONSENT/VEH THEFT|| HIT&RUN PROP DAMAG:LOC/ETC REQ|| OBSTRUCT/ETC PUBLIC OFFICER/ETC
92	NO ARREST RECEIVED|| SEE COMMENT FOR CHARGE
93	CARRY CONCEALED DIRK OR DAGGER|| VIOLATION OF PAROLE:FELONY
	DUI ALCOHOL/DRUGS|| DUI ALCOHOL/0.08 PERCENT|| DRIVE:LIC SUSP/ETC:DUI:SPEC VIOL
	POSSESS CONTROLLED SUBSTANCE
94	PROHIBITED OWN/ETC AMMO/ETC|| VIOLATION OF PAROLE:FELONY
95	PETTY THEFT
	POSSESSION OF ID OF 10+ PRSN: W/ INT DEFRD

ALIEN	CONVICTION(S)
96	PETTY THEFT
	NO ARREST RECEIVED|| SEE COMMENT FOR CHARGE
	666(A)-484(A)-488 PC
97	POSSESS STOLEN VEHICLE/VESSEL/ETC
98	POST RELEASE COMMUNITY SUPV VIOLATION
99	RECEIVE/ETC KNOWN STOLEN PROPERTY
100	POSSESS CONTROLLED SUBSTANCE|| POSSESS CONTROL SUBSTANCE PARAPHERNA
101	POSSESS UNLAW PARAPHERNALIA
102	DRIVING W/LIC INV W/PREV CONV/SUSP/W/O FIN RES
103	FAIL TO ID FUGITIVE INTENT GIVE FALSE INFO
104	PETTY THEFT W/PR JAIL:SPEC OFFENSES
105	BURGLARY|| OBSTRUCT/ETC PUBLIC OFFICER/ETC|| POSSESS UNLAW PARAPHERNALIA
106	DAMAGE PROP-CRIM MISCH
	CONDIT RELEASE VIOLATION
107	CARRY CONCEALED DIRK OR DAGGER
108	POSSESS CONTROL SUBSTANCE PARAPHERNA|| PROBATION VIOL:REARREST/REVOKE
	POSSESS CONTROLLED SUBSTANCE
109	NO ARREST RECEIVED|| SEE COMMENT FOR CHARGE
	POSSESS NARC CONTROL SUBSTANCE
	POSSESS NARC CONTROL SUBSTANCE|| USE/UNDER INFL CONTRLD SUBSTANCE|| POSSESS UNLAW PARAPHERNALIA
110	NO ARREST RECEIVED|| UNSPECIFIED CHARGE
111	211-212,5(A) PC|| 459-460 (A) PC
112	DUI W/PRIOR CONV:PER 23550 VC
113	POSSESS CONTROLLED SUBSTANCE
114	CRIMINAL TRESPASS
115	BURGLARY
	THEFT BY FORGED/INVALID ACCESS CARD
116	RETAIL THEFT
117	TRESPAS OBSTRUC/ETC BUSINES OPR/ETC
	VANDALISM
118	NO ARREST RECEIVED|| GRAND THEFT:MONEY/LABOR/PROP|| SEE COMMENT FOR CHARGE
119	POSSESS CONTROLLED SUBSTANCE|| POSSESS UNLAW PARAPHERNALIA

ALIEN	CONVICTION(S)
	POSSESS CONTROLLED SUBSTANCE|| POSSESS UNLAW PARAPHERNALIA
120	PETTY THEFT W/PR JAIL:SPEC OFFENSES
121	POSSESS UNLAW PARAPHERNALIA
122	POSSESS STOLEN VEHICLE/VESSEL/ETC|| POSS W/INTENT TO USE VEH MASTER KEY
123	OBSTRUCT/RESIST EXECUTIVE OFFICER
124	NO ARREST RECEIVED|| FAIL TO APPEAR AFTER WRITTEN PROMISE
124	NO ARREST RECEIVED|| UNSPECIFIED CHARGE
125	POSS MARIJUANA OVER 28.5 GRAMS|| PROBATION VIOL:REARREST/REVOKE
126	POSSESS CONTROLLED SUBSTANCE
127	OWN/ETC CHOP SHOP|| POSSESS STOLEN VEHICLE/VESSEL/ETC
128	TAKE VEH W/O OWN CONSENT/VEH THEFT|| RECEIVE/ETC KNOWN STOLEN PROPERTY|| POSSESS CONTROL SUBSTANCE PARAPHERNA
129	BURGLARY:SECOND DEGREE|| POSSESS UNLAW PARAPHERNALIA
130	THEFT/PETTY THEFT W/PRIOR|| PROBATION VIOL:REARREST/REVOKE
130	NO ARREST RECEIVED|| POST RELEASE COMMUNITY SUPV VIOLATION
130	NO ARREST RECEIVED|| POST RELEASE COMMUNITY SUPV VIOLATION
131	RECEIVE/ETC KNOWN STOLEN PROPERTY|| POST RELEASE COMMUNITY SUPV VIOLATION
132	CARRY CONCEALED DIRK OR DAGGER
133	NO ARREST RECEIVED|| SEE COMMENT FOR CHARGE
134	EVADE PEACE OFFICER:CAUSE SBI/DEATH|| HIT AND RUN:DEATH OR INJURY|| BURGLARY
135	ASSAULT ON PERSON|| BATTERY
136	GRAND THEFT: MONEY/LABOR/PROP
137	NO ARREST RECEIVED|| TAKE VEH W/O OWN CONSENT/VEH THEFT|| POSSESS STOLEN VEHICLE/VESSEL/ETC
137	NO ARREST RECEIVED|| UNSPECIFIED CHARGE
137	DUI DRUG|| FALSE ID TO PEACE OFFICER
138	INDECENT EXPOSURE|| VIOLATION OF PAROLE:FELONY
139	PETTY THEFT
140	CONTEMPT:VIOL PROTECTIVE ORD/ETC
141	POSSESS CONTROLLED SUBSTANCE
142	DUI ALCOHOL/DRUGS
143	REGISTRATION OF PREDATORY OFFENDERS|| PREDATORY OFFENDER-KNOWINGLY VIOLATES REGISTRATION

ALIEN	CONVICTION(S)
144	NO ARREST RECEIVED‖ SEE COMMENT FOR CHARGE
145	HARM/DEATH:ELDER/DEPENDANT ADULT‖ CONTEMPT:VIOL PROTECTIVE ORD/ETC
145	ROBBERY‖ BURGLARY‖ PROBATION VIOL:REARREST/REVOKE‖ CRUELTY TO ELDER/DEPENDENT ADULT‖ CONTEMPT:VIOL PROTECTIVE ORD/ETC‖ FORCE/ADW NOT FIREARM:GBI LIKELY
146	POSSESS CONTROL SUBSTANCE PARAPHERNA‖ POST RELEASE COMMUNITY SUPV VIOLATION
146	NO ARREST RECEIVED‖ THEFT
147	THEFT-CONTROL PROPERTY
148	INFLICT CORPORAL INJ SPOUSE/COHAB
148	DUI ALCOHOL/DRUGS
149	BATTERY
150	POSSESS NARC CONTROL SUBSTANCE
150	POSSESS NARC CONTROL SUBSTANCE‖ POST RELEASE COMMUNITY SUPV VIOLATION
151	SRV (ILLEGAL RE-ENTERED THE U.S. FND IN CENTRAL CA)
152	LARCENY
153	BATTERY
154	RECEIVE/ETC KNOWN STOLEN PROPERTY‖ POSSESS NARC CONTROL SUBSTANCE‖ POSSESS CONTROL SUBSTANCE PARAPHERNA
155	INDECENT EXPOSURE
156	BURGLARY
157	BATTERY
158	EMER COMM 911 MISUSE
159	EVADE PEACE OFFICER:DISREGARD SAFETY
160	PETTY THEFT
161	NO ARREST RECEIVED‖ SEE COMMENT FOR CHARGE
161	NO ARREST RECEIVED‖ SEE COMMENT FOR CHARGE
162	POSSESS CONTROLLED SUBSTANCE
163	OPERATING WITHOUT A LICENSE ON PERSON
163	CONTROLLED SUBSTANCE-POSSESS (COCAINE, HEROIN
164	FIGHT/NOISE/OFFENSIVE WORDS
164	BURGLARY
165	DRIVE:LIC SUSP/ETC:DUI:SPEC VIOL
166	POSSESS NARC CONTROL SUBSTANCE‖ POSSESS CONTROLLED SUBSTANCE
166	NO ARREST RECEIVED‖ SEE COMMENT FOR CHARGE

ALIEN	CONVICTION(S)
167	EXTREME DUI-BAC > .20
168	DRIVE WHILE LIC SUSPEND/ETC
	TAKE VEH W/O OWN CONSENT/VEH THEFT
	POSSESS CONTROLLED SUBSTANCE
169	TRANSPORT/SELL NARC/CNTL SUB
170	NO ARREST RECEIVED‖ DISORDERLY CONDUCT:INTOX DRUG/ALCOH
171	DRIVE:LIC SUSP/ETC:DUI:SPEC VIOL
172	USE/UNDER INFLUENCE CONTROL SUBST
173	DUI ALCOHOL/DRUGS‖ DUI ALCOHOL/0.08 PERCENT
174	DUI ALCOHOL/DRUGS
175	POSSESS CONTROLLED SUBSTANCE
	POSSESS CONTROLLED SUBSTANCE‖ POSSESS UNLAW PARAPHERNALIA
176	NO ARREST RECEIVED‖ DRIVE W/O LICENSE
177	NO ARREST RECEIVED‖ SEE COMMENT FOR CHARGE
178	DRIVING WHILE LICENSE SUSPENDED OR REVOKED (MISDEMEANOR)
	WILLFUL OBSTRUCTION OF LAW ENFORCEMENT OFFICERS - MISDEMEANOR
	FAILURE TO APPEAR FOR FINGERPRINTABLE CHARGE - MISDEMEANOR
179	NO ARREST RECEIVED‖ SEE COMMENT FOR CHARGE
180	POSSESS CONTROLLED SUBSTANCE‖ USE/UNDER INFL CONTRLD SUBSTANCE‖ POSSESS CONTROL SUBSTANCE PARAPHERNA
181	ASSAULT ON PERSON‖ BATTERY
	NONSTUDENT REFUSE TO LEAVE CAMPUS
	BATTERY ON PERSON
182	DRIVE WHILE LIC SUSPEND/ETC
183	NO ARREST RECEIVED‖ SEE COMMENT FOR CHARGE
184	GET CREDIT/ETC:USE OTHER
	GET CREDIT/ETC:USE OTHER
185	NO ARREST RECEIVED‖ SEE COMMENT FOR CHARGE
186	12500(A) VC
	POSSESS NARC CONTROL SUBSTANCE
	BURGLARY
187	THEFT PROP>=$500 < $1500
188	III/BURGLARY 3RD DEG-UNLAW ENTRY,FEL
189	DISORDERLY CONDUCT
	RESISTING OFFICER

ALIEN	CONVICTION(S)
	BATTERY|| LARCENY
190	BURGLARY
191	DUI ALCOHOL/0.08 PERCENT|| DUI ALCOHOL/DRUGS
192	MANUFAC/POSS/DELIVER SCH 1/II|| POSSESSION OF SCHEDULE 1-V|| CONTROLLED SUBSTANCE CONSPIRACY|| MAN/DEL/POSS/ W/INT/ SCH I/II
193	NO ARREST RECEIVED|| SEE COMMENT FOR CHARGE
194	NO ARREST RECEIVED|| SEE COMMENT FOR CHARGE
195	DUI ALCOHOL/DRUGS
196	VIOLATION OF PAROLE:FELONY
	NO ARREST RECEIVED|| UNSPECIFIED CHARGE
	POSSESS UNLAW PARAPHERNALIA
197	NO ARREST RECEIVED|| SEE COMMENT FOR CHARGE|| TAKE VEH W/O OWN CONSENT/VEH THEFT
198	DRIVE:LIC SUSP/ETC:DUI:SPEC VIOL
199	CONTRACTING W/O A LICENSE
200	CONTEMPT:VIOL GANG INJUNCTION
	CONTEMPT:VIOL GANG INJUNCTION
201	DISORDERLY CONDUCT|| TRAFFIC-DL-DRIVING AFTER CANCELLATION-INIMICAL TO PUBLIC SAFETY
	TRAFFIC-DL-DRIVING AFTER CANCELLATION-INIMICAL TO
202	BURGLARY
203	UNLAWFUL CARRYING WEAPON
204	TRAFFIC - DWI - OPERATE MOTOR VEHICLE UNDER|| DRIVING WHILE IMPAIRED.
205	POSSESS CONTROLLED SUBSTANCE
206	NO ARREST RECEIVED|| SEE COMMENT FOR CHARGE
	VANDALISM
	USE/UNDER INFL CONTRLD SUBSTANCE
207	MAKE/PASS FICTITIOUS CHECK
208	TERRORISTIC THREATS
209	BATTERY
210	RESISTING OFFICER
211	PETTY THEFT RETAIL MERCHANDISE
212	SEXUAL BATTERY
	CHRG 422(A) PC
213	CONTEMPT:DISOBEY COURT ORDER/ETC|| LOCAL ORDINANCE VIOLATION|| FAIL TO APPEAR AFTER WRITTEN PROMISE

ALIEN	CONVICTION(S)
	CONTEMPT:DISOBEY COURT ORDER/ETC|| LOCAL ORDINANCE VIOLATION|| FAIL TO APPEAR AFTER WRITTEN PROMISE
	USE/UNDER INFLUENCE CONTROL SUBST
	USE/UNDER INFLUENCE CONTROL SUBST
	CONTEMPT:DISOBEY COURT ORDER/ETC
214	POSSESS CONCENTRATED CANNABIS
215	TAKE VEH W/O OWN CONSENT/VEH THEFT|| EVADE PEACE OFCR:DISREGARD SAFETY|| GRAND THEFT:AUTO|| RECEIVE/ETC KNOWN STOLEN PROPERTY|| ILLEGAL ENTRY
216	TAKE VEH W/O OWN CONSENT/VEH THEFT
217	BURGLARY: SECOND DEGREE|| GET CREDIT/ETC:USE OTHER
218	FIGHT/NOISE/OFFENSIVE WORDS
219	RETAIL FRAUD - THIRD DEGREE
220	DOM BATTERY, 3+
221	DRIVE WHILE LIC SUSPEND/ETC
	GET CREDIT/ETC:USE OTHER&APOS;S ID|| PROBATION VIOL:REARREST/REVOKE
222	LARCENY
223	COERC W/FORCE OR THREAT OF FORCE
	DESTROY PROP OF ANOTHER, $250 - $5K GROSS MISD
224	LARCENY
225	RECEIVE/ETC KNOWN STOLEN PROPERTY
	POSSESS CONTROLLED SUBSTANCE
	POSSESS CONTROL SUBSTANCE FOR SALE|| POSSESS CONTROLLED SUBSTANCE
	POSSESS CONTROLLED SUBSTANCE
226	INFLICT CORPORAL INJ SPOUSE/COHAB
227	CHRG I415 (2) PC
228	BURGLARY|| TAKE VEH W/O OWN CONSENT/VEH THEFT|| OBSTRUCTS/RESISTS PUBLIC OFFICER/ETC
229	NO ARREST RECEIVED|| SEE COMMENT FOR CHARGE
	PETTY THEFT W/PR JAIL:SPEC OFFENSES|| VIOLATION OF PAROLE:FELONY
230	DRUGS - EQUIP - POSSESS|| DUI-UNLAW BLD ALCH
231	NO ARREST RECEIVED|| POSSESS CONTROLLED SUBSTANCE
232	TAKE VEH W/O OWN CONSENT/VEH THEFT|| RECEIVE/ECT KNOWN STOLEN PROPERTY|| GET CREDIT/ETC:USE OTHER|| POSS DRIVER LIC/ID TO COMMIT FORGERY

ALIEN	CONVICTION(S)
233	FORGE OFFICIAL SEAL
234	DUI ALCOHOL/0.08 PERCENT‖ DRIVE: LIC SUSP/ETC:DUI:SPEC VOIL
	DRIVE WHILE LIC SUSPEND/ETC‖ DUI ALCOHOL/DRUGS
235	DRIVE W/O LICENSE
236	CRIMINAL TRESPASS
	CRIMINAL TRESPASS
237	ASSAULT CAUSES BODILY INJ
238	FORGE ACCESS CARD TO DEFRAUD‖ FELON/ADDICT POSS/ETC FIREARM‖ GET CREDIT/ETC:USE OTHER'S ID‖ FORGE OFFICIAL SEAL
239	CARRY CONCEALED DIRK OR DAGGER‖ OBSTRUCT/ETC PUBLIC OFFICER/ETC‖ POST RELEASE COMMUNITY SUPV VIOLATION
240	FELON/ADDICT POSS/ETC FIREARM
241	POSSESS CONTROLLED SUBSTANCE
242	USE/UNDER INFL CONTRLD SUBSTANCE
243	NO ARREST RECEIVED‖ DRIVE W/O LICENSE
244	RECKLESS DRIVING
245	POSSESS NARC CONTROL SUBSTANCE
	PETTY THEFT W/PR JAIL:SPEC OFFENSES
246	SEE COMMENT FOR CHARGE
247	BURGLARY:SECOND DEGREE
248	USE ACCESS ACCOUNT INFO W/O CONSENT
249	SELL HYPO NEEDLE/SYRINGE W/O PERMIT‖ PROBATION VIOL:REARREST/REVOKE
250	VIOLATION OF PAROLE:FELONY
251	DUI ALCOHOL/0.08 PERCENT
252	SEE COMMENT FOR CHARGE
253	GRAND THEFT: MONEY/LABOR/PROP
254	TAKE VEH W/O OWN CONSENT/VEH THEFT
255	DUI ALCOHOL/DRUGS
256	POSSESS CNTL SUBSTANCE
257	OBSTRUCTS/RESISTS PUBLIC OFFICER/ETC‖ VIOLATION OF PAROLE:FELONY
258	AUTO THEFT W/PRIOR
259	TAKE VEH W/O OWN CONSENT/VEH THEFT
260	POSSESS NARC CONTROL SUBSTANCE
	POSSESS NARC CONTROL SUBSTANCE

ALIEN	CONVICTION(S)
	POSSESS NARC CONTROL SUBSTANCE|| FAIL TO APPEAR AFTER WRITTEN PROMISE
261	POSSESS NARC CONTROL SUBSTANCE|| POSSESS CONTROL SUBSTANCE PARAPHERNA
	POSSESS NARC CONTROL SUBSTANCE
262	MARIJUANA-POSSESS/USE
263	FALSE ID TO SPECIFIC PEACE OFICERS
	NO ARREST RECEIVED|| POSSESS UNLAW PARAPHERNALIA
	NO ARREST RECEIVED|| SEE COMMENT FOR CHARGE
	BURGLARY
264	ILLEGAL ENTRY
265	POSS/PURCHASE FOR SALE NARC/CNTL SUB
266	TRAFFIC OFFENSE
267	DUI ALCOHOL/0.08 PERCENT
268	FLEE/ELUDE POLICE
269	POSSESS MARIJUANA FOR SALE|| PLANT/CULTIVATE/ETC MARIJUANA/HASH
270	NO ARREST RECEIVED|| INFLICT CORPORAL INJ:SPOUSE/COHAB
	NO ARREST RECEIVED|| THREATEN CRIME W/INTENT TO TERRORIZE
271	BURGLARY
272	POSSESS NARC CONTROL SUBSTANCE
273	DUTY TO STOP-ACC.RESULT- DAMG.TO ATT.VEHICLE
	DRIVING AFTER DENIAL, SUS/REVOCATION-LICENSE
274	BATTERY
275	CHRG 3455 PC
276	POSSESS UNLAW PARAPHERNALIA
	BURGLARY
	PROBATION VIOL:REARREST/REVOKE
	BURGLARY|| BURGLARY:SECOND DEGREE
277	TAKE VEH W/O OWN CONSENT/VEH THEFT
278	SIMPLE ASSAULT
279	DISORDERLY CONDUCT:INTOX DRUG/ALCOH
280	SHOPLIFTING-REMOVAL OF GOODS|| SHOPLIFTING-CONCEALMENT|| VIOLATION OF PROMISE TO APPEAR
281	DRIVE WHILE LIC SUPSEND/ETC|| RECKLESS DRIVING
282	TRESPASS:INJURE PROPERTY|| TRANSPORT/SELL NARC/CNTL SUB
	TRANSPORT/SELL NARC/CNTL SUB
283	LARCENY

ALIEN	CONVICTION(S)
284	LARCENY
285	8 USC 1324 ALIEN SMUGGLING
286	POSSESS CONTROLLED SUBSTANCE
	BURGLARY‖ PETTY THEFT W/PR JAIL:SPEC OFFENSES
287	POSS/PURCHASE COCAINE BASE F/SALE
288	VIOL DOM VIOLENCE TPO
289	BURGLARY‖ LARCENY‖ DAMAGE PROP-CRIM MISCH
290	POSS SCH I, II, III, IV C/S, (1ST/2ND)
291	DUI ALCOHOL/0.08 PERCENT
292	ONE COUNT OF 18 USC 111(A)(1)-MISDEMEANOR
293	BAIL JUMPING-FELONY
294	SHOPLIFTING‖ CONTRIB DELINQ/DEPEND OF MINOR
295	FELONY PROSTITUTION
296	POSSESS CONTROLLED SUBSTANCE
297	DRIVE W/O LICENSE
298	CRIM TRESP 3RD DEG/PROPERTY
	DANGEROUS DRUG-POSS/USE
299	CONTRIBUTE DELINQUENCY OF MINOR
300	UNLAWFUL USE/ETC:DRIVER LIC
301	DISORDERLY CONDUCT:INTOX DRUG/ALCOH
302	DRIVE: LIC SUS/ETC: DUI/RFUSE TST
303	NO ARREST RECEIVED‖ DRIVE W/O LICENSE
304	POSSESS CONTROLLED SUBSTANCE
305	NO ARREST RECEIVED‖ DRIVE WHILE LIC SUSPEND/ETC
	NO ARREST RECEIVED‖ DRIVE WHILE LIC SUSPEND/ETC
306	THEFT
	ROBBERY
307	USE/UNDER INFL CONTRLD SUBSTANCE
	OBSTRUCTS/RESISTS PUBLIC OFFICER/ETC
308	ASSAULT
309	BURGLARY‖ RECEIVE/ETC KNOWN STOLEN PROPERTY
310	INFRACTION VIOLATION
311	DRIVE W/O LICENSE
312	BURGLARY‖ BATTERY
313	FALSE ID TO SPECIFIC PEACE OFICERS
314	DUI ALCOHOL/0.08 PERCENT
315	CONTEMPT:DISOBEY COURT ORDER/ETC‖ USE/UNDER INFL CONTRLD SUBSTANCE

ALIEN	CONVICTION(S)
	USE/UNDER INFLUENCE CONTROL SUBST‖ CONTEMPT: DISOBEY COURT ORDER/ETC
316	POSSESS CONTROLLED SUBSTANCE
317	CHRG 422 (A) PC
318	POSSESS CONTROLLED SUBSTANCE
319	DUI/ALCOHOL/0.08 PERCENT
320	FALSE PRETENSES - $200 OR MORE BUT LESS THAN
321	DUI ALCOHOL/0.08 PERCENT
322	ROBBERY WITH DANGEROUS WEAPON
	RECEIVE STOLEN GOODS/PROP (F)
323	BATTERY
324	SEX BATT:TOUCH FOR SEX AROUSAL
325	RECEIVE/ETC KNOWN STOLEN PROPERTY
326	THEFT‖ CHRG 484 (A)-488 PC
	NO ARREST RECEIVED‖ SEE COMMENT FOR CHARGE
327	POSSESS STOLEN VEHICLE/VESSEL/ETC
328	ENTER/ETC NONCOMMERCIAL DWELLING
329	BURGLARY
	BURGLARY
330	BURGLARY
331	AGG DUI-LIC SUSP/REV FOR DUI
332	RAPE SPOUSE BY FORCE/FEAR/ETC
333	POSSESS NARC CONTROL SUBSTANCE
334	OBSTRUCTS/RESISTS PUBLIC OFFICER/ETC‖ CARRY CONCEALED DIRK OR DAGGER
	CARRY CONCEALED DIRK OR DAGGER
335	VIO CS/DRUG/DEV AND COSMETIC ACT
336	BURGLARY:FIRST DEGREE‖ THEFT PERSONAL PROP/PETTY THEFT‖ FALSE ID TO SPECIFIC PEACE OFICERS
337	CONSPIRACY TO HARBOR ALIENS WITHIN THE U.S.
338	POSSESS CONTROLLED SUBSTANCE
339	THEFT
340	DUI/ALCOHOL/0.08 PERCENT
341	POSSESS CONTROLLED SUBSTANCE‖ DRIVE W/O LICENSE‖ FALSE ID TO SPECIFIC PEACE OFFICERS
342	DUI ALCOHOL/0.08 PERCENT
343	UNAUTHORIZED PRESENTMENT OF CARD

ALIEN	CONVICTION(S)
344	CONTEMPT:VIOL GANG INJUNCTION‖ FAIL TO APPEAR AFTER WRITTEN PROMISE
	CHRG 459-460 (A) PC FIRST DEGREE‖ OBSTRUCT/ETC PUBLIC OFFICER/ETC
345	TRESPAS OBSTRUC/ETC BUSINES OPR/ETC
346	DISORDERLY CONDUCT: INTOX DRUG/ALCOH
	BATTERY ON PERSON
347	DRIVE W/O LICENSE‖ USE/UNDER INFL CONTRLD SUBSTANCE
348	LARCENY
349	LARCENY 6
	LARCENY 5
350	DRUG PARAPHERNALIA-POSSESS/USE
	DRUG PARAPHERNALIA-POSSESS/USE ‖RESIST ARREST -PASSV RESISTANCE
351	FINANCIAL TRANSACTION CARD FRAUD-USE-NO CONSENT
352	DISORDERLY CONDUCT‖ ASSAULT-5TH DEGREE-FEAR OF BODILY HARM OR DEATH
	ASSAULT-5TH DEGREE-FEAR OF BODILY HARM OR DEATH
353	DRIVING WHILE LICENSE SUSPENDED OR REVOKED (MISDEMEANOR)
354	DRIVING WHILE INTOXICATED 2ND
355	POSSESS CONTROLLED SUBSTANCE‖ POSSESS UNLAW PARAPHERNALIA
	POSSESS UNLAW PARAPHERNALIA
356	POSSESS NARC CONTROL SUBSTANCE
357	FRAUD‖ LARCENY
358	RESID MORTGAGE FRAUD
359	ROBBERY
360	BURGLARY‖ PAROLE VIOL-FLASH INCARCERATION
	NO ARREST RECEIVED‖ PAROLE VIOL-FLASH INCARCERATION
361	SHOPLIFTING-REMOVAL OF GOODS‖ CRIMINAL TRESPASS 2ND DEGREE‖ ASSAULT-TOUCHED TO INJURE
	CRIM TRESP 3RD DEG/PROPERTY
	SHOPLIFTING-REMOVAL OF GOODS
	CRIMINAL TRESPASS 2ND DEG
362	POSSESSION OF FIREARM BY FELON‖ ASSAULT WITH A DEADLY WEAPON
363	TRAFFIC - DWI - FOURTH-DEGREE DRIVING WHILE‖ ASSAULT IN THE 5TH DEG
	FINANCIAL TRANSACTION CARD FRAUD-USE-NO CONSENT

ALIEN	CONVICTION(S)
	FINANCIAL TRANSACTION CARD FRAUD-USE-NO CONSENT‖ DRUGS - 5TH DEGREE - POSSESS SCHEDULE 1,2,3,4 -
364	SIMPLE ROBBERY
	THEFT-TAKE/USE/TRANSFER MOVABLE PROP-NO CONSENT
365	DUI ALCOHOL/DRUGS
366	CHRG 490,1 PC
367	FAIL PROVE FIN RSP: PO REQUEST
368	LOITER:INTENT:PROSTITUTION‖ FAIL TO APPEAR AFTER WRITTEN PROMISE
	LOITER:INTENT:PROSTITUTION
	LOITER:INTENT:PROSTITUTION‖ FAIL TO APPEAR AFTER WRITTEN PROMISE
369	MOVING TRAFFIC VIOL‖ REFUSAL TO SUBMIT TO BREATH/BLOOD/OR URINE TEST‖ DRIVING WHILE LIC SUSP 1ST OFF
370	FALSE IMPRISONMENT/INFLICT CORPORAL INJ SPOUSE/COHAB
371	SHOPLIFT-LESS PURCHASE PRICE
372	DRIVE W/O LICENSE‖ DUI ALCOHOL/DRUGS
373	BATTERY ON PERSON
374	DRIVE W/LIC SUSP/REVOKE/CANC
375	PROSTITUTION-PATRON-HIRES, OFFERS, OR AGREES TO
376	FRAUD TO OBTAIN AID
377	POSS WPN BY PROHIB PERSON
378	FAIL REGISTER SEX OFFENDER(F)‖ INDECENT LIBERTY WITH CHILD
379	NO ARREST RECEIVED‖ DRIVE:LIC SUSP/ETC:DUI:SPEC VIOL
380	HIT AND RUN:PROPERTY DAMAGE‖ DUI ALCOHOL/0.08 PERCENT
381	LARCENY‖ BURGLARY
382	POSSESS CONTROLLED SUBSTANCE
383	VANDALISM
384	FLEEING A PEACE OFFICER BY A MEANS OTHER THAN A
385	DRIVE: UNDER INFLUENCE ALCOHOL
386	NO ARREST RECEIVED‖ DRIVE WHILE LIC SUSPEND/ETC
387	BATTERY ON PERSON
388	EXTREME DUI-BAC > .20
389	DUI ALCOHOL/DRUGS‖ DUI ALCOHOL/0.08 PERCENT‖ DRIVE W/O LICENSE
390	THEFT
	BURGLARY
391	FAIL TO COMPLY-COURT ORDER‖ FAIL TO STAY/ACCID/ATTEND VEH

ALIEN	CONVICTION(S)
392	POSSESS STOLEN VEHICLE/VESSEL/ETC‖ TAKE VEH W/O OWN CONSENT/VEH THEFT
393	DRIVE W.O LICENSE
394	DRIVE W/LIC SUSP/REVOKE/CANC
395	BRAWLING FIGHTING CORRUPT PUBLIC MORAL DECENY
396	CARRY CONCEALED DIRK AND DAGGER‖ USE/UNDER INFL CONTRLD SUBSTANCE
	USE/UNDER INFL CONTRLD SUBSTANCE‖ DEPORTATION PROCEEDINGS
397	NO ARREST RECEIVED‖ SEE COMMENT FOR CHARGE
398	USE/UNDER INFL CONTRLD SUBSTANCE
	POSSESS CONTROLLED SUBSTANCE
399	TRAFFIC OFFENSE‖ MOVING TRAFFIC VIOL
400	ROBBERY
401	POSSESS CONTROLLED SUBSTANCE‖ PROBATION VIOL:REARREST/REVOKE‖ USE/UNDER INFL CONTRLD SUBSTANCE
402	BURGLARY‖ MISUSE OF 911 OR E911 SYSTEM
403	RETAIL THEFT/DISP MERCH/<$300
404	VIO CS/DRUG/DEV AND COSMETIC ACT
405	NO ARREST RECEIVED‖ FAIL TO APPEAR AFTER WRITTEN PROMISE
406	DRIVING AFTER DENIAL, SUS/REVOCATION-LICENSE‖ FAILURE TO APPEAR/ANSWER SUMMONS
407	DRIVE:LIC SUSP/ETC:DUI:SPEC VIOL
408	DISORDERLY CONDUCT:PROSTITUTION
409	NONMOVING TRAFFIC VIOL
410	SX OFF FAIL ANNUAL UPDATE
411	III/DANGEROUS DRUG-POSS/USE CHANGED TO DANGEROUS DRUG VIOLATION,FEL
412	DISORDERLY CONDUCT:INTOX DRUG/ALCOH‖ OBSTRUCT/ETC PUBLIC OFFICER/ETC
413	TRESPASSING
	FIGHT/CHALLENGE FIGHT
	NO ARREST RECEIVED‖ THEFT/PETTY THEFT
	NO ARREST RECEIVED‖ THEFT/PETTY THEFT
414	DUI ALCOHOL/DRUGS
415	DUI ALCOHOL/0.08 PERCENT‖ DRIVE:LIC SUSP/ETC:DUI:SPEC VIOL
416	DISORDERLY CONDUCT:INTOX DRUG/ALCOH‖ POSSESS CONTROL SUBSTANCE FOR SALE‖ RECEIVE/ETC KNOWN STOLEN PROPERTY
417	PETTY THEFT RETAIL MERCHANDISE/ETC

ALIEN	CONVICTION(S)
418	TRANSPORT/ETC CNTL SUB
419	UNLAWFUL USE/ETC:DRIVER LIC
420	VANDALISM‖ FAIL TO APPEAR AFTER WRITTEN PROMISE
	BATTERY
421	THREATEN CRIME WITH INTENT TO TERRORIZE‖ CRIM STREET GANG:W/PUB OFF CONV
422	INFRACTION
423	POSSESS CONTROLLED SUBSTANCE
424	POSSESS CONTROLLED SUBSTANCE‖ FAIL TO APPEAR:WRITTEN PROMISE
425	DOM BATTERY, 1ST
426	SEE COMMENT FOR CHARGE
427	POSSESS CONTROLLED SUBSTANCE
428	TRESPASS:RAILROAD PROPERTY
429	DUI ALCOHOL/0.08 PERCENT‖ DUI ALCOHOL/DRUGS
430	BAT:SPOUSE/EX SP/DATE/ETC
431	DUI ALCOHOL/DRUGS
432	DRIVE:LIC SUSP/ETC:DUI:SPEC VIOL
433	NO ARREST RECEIVED‖ DRIVE:LIC SUSP/ETC:DUI:SPEC VIOL
434	NONMOVING TRAFFIC VIOL
	NONMOVING TRAFFIC VIOL
435	FAIL DISCLOSE ORIGIN RECORDING
436	FALSE IDENT TO LAW ENFORCEMENT‖ CRIMINAL TRESPASS
	CRIMINAL TRESPASS
437	RETAIL THEFT
438	ROBBERY
439	LOCAL ORDINANCE VIOLATION
440	DRIVE:LIC SUSP/ETC:DUI:SPEC VIOL
441	CHILD CRUELTY:POS INJURY/DEATH
442	ASSAULT
443	DRIVE:LIC SUSP/ETC:DUI:SPEC VIOL
444	TRAN FAIL 30 DAY UPDATE
445	CONTEMPT:DISOBEY COURT ORDER/ETC
446	RETAIL THEFT - INTENTIONALLY TAKE
447	NO ARREST RECEIVED‖ SEE COMMENT FOR CHARGE
	THEFT
448	BURGLARY

ALIEN	CONVICTION(S)
449	ASSAULT-5TH-SAME VICTIM-TWO OR MORE PREVIOUS‖ ASSAULT IN THE FIFTH DEGREE; GROSS MISDEMEANOR-
450	ROBBERY
451	FRAUD
452	MOVING TRAFFIC VIOL
	MOVING TRAFFIC VIOL
453	DUI-UNLAW BLD ALCH
454	NO ARREST RECEIVED‖ DISORDERLY CONDUCT:INTOX DRUG/ALCOH
455	HIT AND RUN:PROPERTY DAMAGE‖ DRIVE:SUSPENDED/ETC LIC:RECKLESS‖ DRIVE:LIC SUS/ETC:DUI/RFUSE TST‖ DRIVE:LIC SUSP/ETC:DUI:SPEC VIOL
456	LARCENY 6
457	PETTY THEFT
458	TAKE VEH W/O OWN CONSENT/VEH THEFT
459	CONSPIRACY:COMMIT CRIME‖ RECEIVE/ETC KNOWN STOLEN PROPERTY
460	NO ARREST RECEIVED‖ ENTER/REMAIN ON POSTED PROPERTY
461	POSSESS CONTROLLED SUBSTANCE
462	DRIVE:LIC SUSP/ETC:DUI:SPEC VIOL
463	SEE COMMENT FOR CHARGE
464	SEE COMMENT FOR CHARGE
465	POSSESS CONTROLLED SUBSTANCE
466	OBSTRUCT/ETC PUBLIC OFFICER/ETC‖ FAIL TO APPEAR AFTER WRITTEN PROMISE
467	POSSESS CONTROLLED SUBSTANCE
468	NO ARREST RECEIVED‖ DRIVE WHILE LIC SUSPEND/ETC
469	NO ARREST RECEIVED‖ DRIVE W/O LICENSE
470	POSSESS CONTROLLED SUBSTANCE‖ POSSESS UNLAW PARAPHERNALIA
	POSSESS CONTROLLED SUBSTANCE‖ POSSESS UNLAW PARAPHERNALIA
471	BRING CONTROL SUB/ETC INTO PRISON/ETC‖ POSSESS CONTROLLED SUBSTANCE
472	LOITER:INTENT:PROSTITUTION
473	DISTURBS BY LOUD/UNREASONABLE NOISE
474	DUI ALCOHOL/DRUGS‖ DUI ALCOHOL/0.08 PERCENT
475	DUI ALCOHOL/DRUGS
476	POSSESS CONTROLLED SUBSTANCE‖ USE/UNDER INFL CONTRLD SUBSTANCE

ALIEN	CONVICTION(S)
477	TRANSPORT/ETC CONTROL SUBSTANCE
478	DUI ALCOHOL/DRUGS
479	8 USC 1325-ILLEGAL ENTRY (M)
480	NO ARREST RECEIVED‖ DRIVE W/O LICENSE
	RECEIVE/ETC KNOWN STOLEN PROPERTY
	BURGLARY‖ CONSPIRACY:COMMIT CRIME‖ POSSESS/ETC BURGLARY TOOLS
481	8 USC 1325 ILLEGAL ENTRY (M)
482	NO ARREST RECEIVED‖ SEE COMMENT FOR CHARGE‖ PARTICIPATE:CRIMINAL STREET GANG
483	DRIVE WHILE LIC SUSPEND/ETC
484	POSSESS NARC CONTROL SUBSTANCE
485	DRIVE:LIC SUSP/ETC:DUI:SPEC VIOL
486	POSSESS CONCENTRATED CANNABIS‖ OBSTRUCT/ETC PUBLIC OFFICER/ETC‖ DESTROY/CONCEAL EVIDENCE
	CHILD CRUELTY:POS INJURY/DEATH
487	INFLICT CORPORAL INJ SPOUSE/COHAB
	BAT:SPOUSE/EX SP/DATE/ETC‖ VIO CRT ORD TO PREVNT DOMESTC VIOL
488	INFLICT CORPORAL INJ SPOUSE/COHAB
489	BAT:SPOUSE/EX SP/DATE/ETC
490	PROBATION VIOLATION REFERENCE OBT 4804060529
491	DRUG PARAPHERNALIA-POSSESS/USE
492	DISORDERLY CONDUCT:INTOX DRUG/ALCOH‖ FAIL TO APPEAR AFTER WRITTEN PROMISE
	DISORDERLY CONDUCT:INTOX DRUG/ALCOH
	SEE COMMENT FOR CHARGE
	ARSON:PROPERTY
493	DUI .08 ALCOHOL:CAUSE BODILY INJ
494	DUI - FIRST OFFENSE DUI‖ MOTOR VEHICLE VIOLATION - NO LICENSE‖ FAILURE OF OWNER OR OPERATOR OF MOTOR VEHICLE
495	RESISTING PUBLIC OFFICER
496	ATTEMPTED COMMON LAW ROBBERY
	COMMON LAW ROBBERY
	COMMON LAW ROBBERY
497	OPERATING WHILE REVOKED
	OPERATE W/O CARRYING LICENSE
	OPERATING WHILE REVOKED

ALIEN	CONVICTION(S)
498	HIT AND RUN: PROPERTY DAMAGE
499	BURGLARY
	POSSESS CONTROL SUBSTANCE PARAPHERNA
	NO ARREST RECEIVED‖ SEE COMMENT FOR CHARGE
	RECEIVE/ETC KNOWN STOLEN PROPERTY
500	THEFT - MOTOR VEHICLE DEFINED‖ THEFT-TAKE/DRIVE MOTOR VEHICLE-NO OWNER CONSENT
501	AGGRAVATED ASSAULT‖ CRIMINAL DAMAGE
502	8 USC 1325A1 IMPROPER ENTRY OF ALIEN; CONCEALMENT OF FACTS; MARRIAGE FRAUD
503	PROBATION VIOLATION REFERENCE OBT 1102045384
504	MARIJUANA-POSSESS
	MARIJUANA-POSSESS
505	NO ARREST RECEIVED‖ DRIVE W/O LICENSE
506	PETTY THEFT
507	BURGLARY
508	OBSTRUCTION-REFUSE TRUE NAME
509	GRAND THEFT:AUTO
510	POSSESS CONTROLLED SUBSTANCE
511	FRAUD‖ PASS FORGED
512	LOUD/UNREASONABLE NOISE
513	PROBATION VIOLATION
	PROBATION VIOLATION REFERENCE OBT 1101092442‖ PROBATION VIOLATION REFERENCE OBT 1101094288
514	DRIVE:LIC SUSP/ETC:DUI:SPEC VIOL
515	LARCENY
516	BATTERY
517	TRESPASSING/ CRIMINAL POSSESSION STOLEN PROPERTY-5TH DEGREE
518	POSSESS NARC CONTROL SUBSTANCE
519	DRUGS-POSSESS‖ MARIJUANA-POSSESS‖ DRUGS - EQUIP - POSSESS
520	POSSESSION OF BURGLARY OR THEFT TOOLS
521	DRIVING W/O LICENSE
522	CRIMINAL TRESPASS
523	DISORDERLY CONDUCT
	TRAFFIC - DWI - OPERATE MOTOR VEHICLE - ALCOHOL
524	DUI OF ALCOHOL OR CONTRL SUBST

ALIEN	CONVICTION(S)
525	BURGLARY
526	DUI ALCOHOL/0.08 PERCENT
527	CRIMINAL TRESPASS-BLDG AND OCCUP
528	VIO CRT ORD TO PREVNT DOMESTC VIOL
529	DUI ALCOHOL/DRUGS
530	FRAUD-ILLEG USE CREDIT CARDS‖ FRAUD-IMPERSON
531	POSSESS UNLAW PARAPHERNALIA
532	DRIVE W/LIC SUSP/REVOKE/CANC
	DRIVE W/LIC SUSP/REVOKE/CANC
533	THEFT PROP>=$50 < $500
534	INFLICT CORPORAL INJ ON SPOUSE/COHAB
535	NO ARREST RECEIVED‖ DRIVE WHILE LIC SUSPEND/ETC
536	NO ARREST RECEIVED‖ DUI W/PRIOR CONV:PER 23550 VC‖ DUI 0.08%W/PRS:PER 23550VC‖ AIDE/ABET IN EXHIBITION OF SPEED‖ DRIVE:LIC SUSP/ETC:DUI:SPEC VIOL‖ RECKLESS DRIVING:HIGHWAY
537	FORCE/ADW NOT FIREARM:GBI LIKELY
	USE/UNDER INFL CONTRLD SUBSTANCE
538	POSSESS CONTROLLED SUBSTANCE
539	NO ARREST RECEIVED‖ DRIVE W/O LICENSE
	NO ARREST RECEIVED‖ DRIVE W/O LICENSE
	ASSAULT ON PERSON‖ BATTERY
540	TAKE VEH W/O OWN CONSENT/VEH THEFT
541	BATTERY
542	USE/UNDER INFL CONTRLD SUBSTANCE
543	EMBEZZLEMENT
544	DWI - LEVEL/ NO OPERATORS LICENSE
545	ASSAULT CAUSES BODILY INJ‖ POSS CS PG 1 < 1G
546	8 USC 1325 ILLEGAL ENTRY (M)
547	8 USC 1325-ILLEGAL ENTRY
548	FALSE ID TO SPECIFIC PEACE OFICERS
549	BATTERY
	TAKE VEH W/O OWN CONSENT/VEH THEFT
550	TAKE VEH W/O OWN CONSENT/VEH THEFT
551	OBSTRUCT/ETC PUBLIC OFFICER/ETC
552	POSSESS CONTROLLED SUBSTANCE‖ POSSESS CONTROL SUBSTANCE PARAPHERNA‖ USE/UNDER INFLUENCE CONTROL SUBST
553	DRIVE W/O LICENSE CONVICTION

ALIEN	CONVICTION(S)
554	DRIVE W/LIC SUSP/REVOKE/CANC
	8 USC 1325 ILLEGAL ENTYR (M)
555	LARCENY
556	RESISTING OFFICER
557	RECKLESS DRIVING
558	DUI ALCOHOL/0.08 PERCENT
559	DUI ALCOHOL/0.08 PERCENT‖ DRIVE:LIC SUSP/ETC:DUI:SPEC VIOL
560	DRIVING WHILE INTOXICATED
561	FORGERY-OFFERS FORGED INSTRUM/TAKING IDENTITY OF ANOTHER/CRIM IMPERSONATION-FALSE ID
562	RESISTING OFFICER
	TRESPASSING
563	OPERATING - LICENSE SUSPENDED, REVOKED, DENIED
564	DUI ALCOHOL/DRUGS
565	INFLICT CORPORAL INJ SPOUSE/COHAB
566	DRIVING WHILE INTOXICATED
567	DISORDERLY CONDUCT‖ PROBATION VIOLATION
568	ILLEGAL ENTRY
569	OBSTRUCT/ETC PUBLIC OFFICER/ETC
570	TRESPASS: PRIVATE PROPERTY
571	BATTERY
572	NO ARREST RECEIVED‖ HIT AND RUN:PROPERTY DAMAGE‖ DRIVE W/O LICENSE
573	DRIVE WHILE LIC SUSPEND/ETC‖ DUI ALCOHOL/0.08 PERCENT
574	BURGLARY
575	POSSESS CONTROLLED SUBSTANCE
576	NO ARREST RECEIVED‖ DRIVE WHILE LIC SUSPEND/ETC
577	NO ARREST RECEIVED‖ OBSTRUCT/ETC PUBLIC OFFICER/ETC
578	CHILD/VUL ADULT ABUSE-INTENT
579	ILLEGAL ENTRY
580	EXTREME DUI-BAC .15-.20
581	DRIVE W/LIC SUSP/REVOKE/CANC
582	POSSESS CONTROLLED SUBSTANCE‖ POSSESS UNLAW PARAPHERNALIA‖ POSS MARIJUANA 28.5- GRAMS
	FELON/ADDICT POSS/ETC FIREARM/POSSESS NARC CONTROL SUBSTANCE
583	DISORDERLY CONDUCT:INTOX DRUG/ALCOH
	BATTERY

ALIEN	CONVICTION(S)
584	NO ARREST RECEIVED‖ CHARGE NOT SPECIFIED
585	DRIVING WHILE INTOXICATED W/CHILD UNDER 15 YOA
586	FALSE ID TO SPECIFIC PEACE OFFICERS
587	POSSESS CONTROLLED SUBSTANCE
588	NO ARREST RECEIVED‖ DUI ALCOHOL/DRUGS‖ DUI ALCOHOL/0.08 PERCENT‖ DRIVE W/O LICENSE‖ DRIVE:LIC SUSP/ETC:DUI:SPEC VIOL‖ DRIVE:LIC SUS/ETC:DUI/RFUSE TST
589	DRIVE W/O LICENSE
590	DUI ALCOHOL
591	BURGLARY:FIRST DEGREE‖ PARTICIPATE IN CRIM STREET GANG‖ PROBATION VIOL:REARREST/REVOKE
592	NO ARREST RECEIVED‖ SEE COMMENT FOR CHARGE
592	INFLICT COPORAL INJ SPOUSE/COHAB/VIOL PROTECT ORD:DOMESTIC:W/PR
593	RESISTING OFFICER
594	NONMOVING TRAFFIC VIOL
595	NO ARREST RECEIVED‖ DRIVE W/O LICENSE
596	DUI ALCOHOL/0.08 PERCENT
597	DUI ALCOHOL/0.08 PERCENT
598	RECKLESS DRIVING
599	OPERATING - NO LICENSE/MULTIPLE LICENSES
600	OPERATING - LICENSE SUSPENDED, REVOKED, DENIED
601	OPERATING-NO LICENSE FOR THREE YEARS 1ST OFFENSE
602	MALICIOUS DESTRUCTION OF PERSONAL PROPERTY-$200
603	FALSE IDENTIFICATION TO PEACE OFFICER/DRIVE:LIC SUS/ECT:DUI/RFUSE TST
603	DRIVE:LIC SUS/ETC:DUI/RFUSE TST‖ FALSE ID TO SPECIFIC PEACE OFICERS‖ BENCH WARRANT:FTA:MISDEMEANOR CHARGE‖ DUI ALCOHOL
604	DRIVE WHILE LIC SUSPEND
605	BURGLARY
605	BURGLARY:SECOND DEGREE‖ CONSPIRACY:COMMIT CRIME
606	NO ARREST RECEIVED‖ DRIVE WHILE LIC SUSPEND/ETC
607	OBSTRUCT/ETC PUBLIC OFFICER/ETC‖ VIO CRT ORD TO PREVNT DOMESTC VIOL
608	DUI ALCOHOL/0.08 PERCENT/DRIVE:LIC SUS/ETC:DUI/RFUSE TST
609	DRIVING WITHOUT A VALID LICENSE (MISDEMEANOR)
610	GRAND LARCENY < $3500

ALIEN	CONVICTION(S)
611	DRIVING WHILE INTOXICATED|| EVADING ARREST DETENTION|| RESIST ARREST SEARCH OR TRANSP
612	VIO CRT ORD TO PREVNT DOMESTC VIOL
613	NO ARREST RECEIVED|| DRIVE W/O LICENSE
614	SHOW ON VEH/GIVE OFFICER UNLAWF REG|| DRIVE W/O LICENSE
615	TRESPASSING
616	THEFT BY UNLWF TAKING OR DISPO|| FALSE IDENT TO LAW ENFORCEMENT
617	THEFT-FALSE REPRESENTATION
618	POSSESS DRUG PARAPHERNALIA
619	OPERATE W/O CARRYING LICENSE
620	SF-946.41 - OBSTRUCTING|| SF-947.01 - DISORDERLY CONDUCT
621	RESISTING OR OBSTRUCTING AN OFFICER
622	OPERATING WHILE UNDER INFLUENCE
623	POSSESSION OF MARIJUANA|| OBSTRUCTING OFFICER
624	OPERATE W/O CARRYING LICENSE
625	11.947.01 DISORDERLY CONDUCT
626	RESISTING OR OBSTRUCTING AN OFFICER
627	OPERATING WHILE REVOKED
628	RECKLESS DRIVING
629	DUI .08 ALCOHOL:CAUSE BODILY INJ
630	DUI ALCOHOL
631	DUI ALCOHOL/0.08 PERCENT|| DRIVE:LIC SUSP/ETC:DUI:SPEC VIOL
632	DUI ALCOHOL/0.08 PERCENT/DRIVE:LIC SUS/ETC:DUI:SPEC VIOL
633	RECKLESS DRIVING
634	THEFT (484)
635	TAKE VEH W/O OWN CONSENT (10851 (A) VC)
636	INFLICT CORPORAL INJ ON SPOUSE/COHAB|| WILLFUL CRUELTY TO CHILD|| LOCAL ORDINANCE VIOLATION
637	RESISTING OFFICER
638	RECKLESS DRIVING TO ENDANGER|| DWI - LEVEL 4
639	LARCENY
640	INJURY TO PERSONAL PROPERTY|| RECKLESS DRIVING TO ENDANGER|| RECKLESS DRVG-WANTON DISREGARD|| HIT/RUN LEAVE SCENE PROP DAM
641	8 USC 1325A1 ENTRY WITHOUT INSPECTION, TIME OR PLACE NOT DESIGNATED
642	ASSAULT ON A FEMALE

ALIEN	CONVICTION(S)
643	OBTAIN PROPERTY FALSE PRETENSE||OBTAIN PROPERTY FALSE PRETENSE
	POSS STOLEN GOODS/PROP (F)|| OBTAIN PROPERTY FALSE PRETENSE||FORGERY OF INSTRUMENT
	POSS STOLEN GOODS/PROP (F)|| OBTAIN PROPERTY FALSE PRETENSE|| FORGERY OF INSTRUMENT
	OBTAIN PROPERTY FALSE PRETENSE
	OBTAIN PROPERTY FALSE PRETENSE
644	DRIVE:LIC SUSP/ETC:DUI:SPEC VIOL|| DUI ALCOHOL/0.08 PERCENT|| CONTEMPT:DISOBEY COURT ORDER/ETC
645	DRUG PARAPHERNALIA-POSSESS/USE||DRUG PARAPHERNALIA-POSSESS/USE
646	BURGLARY, (1ST)|| PETIT LARCENY
647	SHOPLIFTING-REMOVAL OF GOODS
	MARIJUANA-POSSESS/USE
648	TRAFFIC - DWI - OPERATE MOTOR VEHICLE - ALCOHOL
649	EVADING ARREST DETENTION
650	FLEE/ELUDE ARREST W/MV (M)
	RESISTING PUBLIC OFFICER
651	OBSTRUCT/ETC PUBLIC OFFICER/ETC (148(A)(1) PC)||OBSTRUCT/ETC PUBLIC OFFICER/ETC (148(A)(1) PC)
652	INTRFERE/RESIST|| LOITER SCHOOL
653	POSSESS CONTROLLED SUBSTANCE|| POSSESS UNLAW PARAPHERNALIA
654	BAT:SPOUSE/EX SP/DATE/ETC (243(E)(1) PC)||BAT:SPOUSE/EX SP/DATE/ETC (243(E)(1) PC)
	POSSESS/ETC BURGLARY TOOLS
655	DUI ALCOHOL/0.08 PERCENT||DRIVE:LIC SUSP/ETC:DUI:SPEC VIOL
656	DRIVE:LIC SUSP/ETC:DUI:SPEC VIOL
657	DISTURBS BY LOUD/UNREASONABLE NOISE ILLEGAL SPEED CONTEST
658	POSSESS NARC CONTROL SUBSTANCE|| POSSESS CONTROL SUBSTANCE PARAPHERNA
659	LOUD/UNREASONABLE NOISE
660	DUI ALCOHOL/DRUGS
661	CCW ON PERSON|| ROBBERY
662	DUI ALCOHOL/0.08 PERCENT

ALIEN	CONVICTION(S)
663	RECKLESS DRIVING
664	POSSESS CONTROLLED SUBSTANCE|| POSSESS CONTROL SUBSTANCE PARAPHERNA
665	CHRG 71,03(D) MC
666	ACT AS DEALR/MANUFACTURER/ETC W/O LIC
667	DRIVE W/O LICENSE (12500(A) VC)
668	CARRY CONCEALED DIRK OR DAGGER
669	DRIVE:LIC SUSP/ETC:DUI:SPEC VIOL (14601.2(A) VC
670	PETTY THEFT
671	POSSESS CONTROLLED SUBSTANCE
672	FORGERY|| INFLICT CORPORAL INJ:SPOUSE/COHAB|| BATTERY
673	TAKE VEH W/O OWN CONSENT/VEH THEFT
674	ASSAULT WITH FIREARM ON PERSON
675	ENT/ETC NONCOM DWELL:INCIDENT||WILLFUL CRUELTY TO CHILD ARSON:PROPERTY
676	FORGE OFFICIAL SEAL
677	POSSESS CONTROLLED SUBSTANCE
678	INFLICT CORPORAL INJ SPOUSE/COHAB
679	DRIVE W/O LICENSE
	TAKE VEH W/O OWN CONSENT/VEH THEFT
680	OBSTRUCT/RESIST EXECUTIVE OFFICER
681	DUI ALCOHOL/0.08 PERCENT
682	VANDALISM
683	ROBBERY:SECOND DEGREE||
684	ASSAULT:W/INTENT TO RAPE
685	NO ARREST RECEIVED|| DRIVE W/O LICENSE
686	POSS MARIJUANA 28.5- GRAMS|| RECEIVE/ETC KNOWN STOLEN PROPERTY
	BURGLARY
	CONTEMPT:DISOBEY COURT ORDER/ETC|| USE FALSE CITIZENSHIP/ETC DOCUMENTS|| RECEIVE/ETC KNOWN STOLEN PROPERTY
687	DUI ALCOHOL/DRUGS|| DUI ALCOHOL/0.08 PERCENT
688	OBSTRUCT/ETC PUBLIC OFFICER/ETC
689	DRIVE WHILE LIC SUSPEND/ETC
690	NO ARREST RECEIVED|| TRESPASS:RAILROAD PROPERTY
691	POSSESS NARC CONTROL SUBSTANCE|| POSSESS UNLAW PARAPHERNALIA
692	NO ARREST RECEIVED|| DRIVE W/O LICENSE

ALIEN	CONVICTION(S)
693	NO ARREST RECEIVED‖ DRIVE W/O LICENSE
694	NO ARREST RECEIVED‖ DRIVE W/O LICENSE
695	NO ARREST RECEIVED‖ FAIL TO APPEAR AFTER WRITTEN PROMISE
	NO ARREST RECEIVED‖ FAIL TO APPEAR AFTER WRITTEN PROMISE
696	CHRG 459-460(B) PC SECOND DEGREE
697	NO ARREST RECEIVED‖ DRIVE:LIC SUSP/ETC:DUI:SPEC VIOL
698	LIC SUSP/ETC:DUI:SPEC VIOL
699	CONTEMPT:VIOL PROTECTIVE ORD/ETC
700	DRIVE WHILE LIC SUSPEND/ETC
	POSSESS CONTROLLED SUBSTANCE
701	NO ARREST RECEIVED‖ DRIVE W/O LICENSE
702	DUI:ALCOHOL/DRUGS
703	NO ARREST RECEIVED‖ DRIVE WHILE LIC SUSPEND/ETC
704	NO ARREST RECEIVED‖ DRIVE W/O LICENSE
705	NO ARREST RECEIVED‖ POSS DRILL/ETC:INT VANDALISM/ETC
706	BURGLARY‖ POSSESS UNLAW PARAPHERNALIA
707	NO ARREST RECEIVED‖ DRIVE WHILE LIC SUSPEND/ETC
708	DUI ALCOHOL/0.08 PERCENT‖ DUI ALCOHOL/DRUGS‖ DRIVE W/O LICENSE
	NO ARREST RECEIVED‖ DRIVE:LIC SUS/ETC:DUI/RFUSE TST
709	DUI ALCOHOL/DRUGS‖ DUI ALCOHOL/0.08 PERCENT‖ DRIVE W/O LICENSE
710	NO ARREST RECEIVED‖ DISORDERLY CONDUCT:PROSTITUTION
711	CONTEMPT:VIOL PROTECTIVE ORD/ETC
712	1. DRIVER: LIC SUS/ETC:DUI/RFUSE TST; 2. DUI ALCOHOL/0.08 PERCENT
713	NO ARREST RECEIVED‖ DRIVE:LIC SUS/ETC:DUI/RFUSE TST
714	DUI ALCOHOL/0.08 PERCENT
715	DRIVE: LIC SUSP/ETC:DUI:SPEC VIOL
716	GRAND THEFT FROM PERSON
717	8 USC 1325A1 ENTRY WITHOUT INSPECTION, TIME OR PLACE NOT DESIGNATED
718	NONMOVING TRAFFIC VIOL
719	MOVING TRAFFIC VIOL
720	NONMOVING TRAFFIC VIOL
721	DUI ALCOHOL
722	POSSESS CONTROLLED SUBSTANCE
723	DUI ALCOHOL/DRUGS
724	INFLICT CORPORAL INJ SPOUSE/COHAB

ALIEN	CONVICTION(S)
725	DRIVING WHILE LICENSE SUSPENDED OR REVOKED (MISDEMEANOR)
726	1. AGG ASLT-OFFICER; 2. RESIST ARREST-PHYSICAL FORCE
727	POSS <= 1OZ MARIJUANA, (1ST)
728	DRIVE W/LIC SUSP/REVOKE/CANC
729	DUI-LIQUOR/DRUGS/VAPORS/COMBO
730	EXTREME DUI-BAC .15 OR MORE
731	DANGEROUS DRUG VIOLATION
732	AGG DUI-LIC SUSP/REV FOR DUI
	EXTREME DUI-BAC .15 OR MORE
733	FAIL TO SHOW DRIV LIC OR ID
734	1. THEFT-CONTROL PROPERTY; 2. BURGLARY 2ND DEGREE
735	DRIVE W/LIC SUSP/REVOKE/CANC‖ FAIL TO SHOW DRIV LIC OR ID
	DRIVE W/LIC SUSP/REVOKE/CANC
736	VIO CS/DRUG/DEV AND COSMETIC ACT
737	1. 8 USC 1182 ALIEN INADMISSIBILITY UNDER SECTIN 212; 2. 8 USC 13251A1 ENTRY WITHOUT INSPECTIN, TIME OR PLACE NOT DESIGNATED
738	DRIVING WHILE LICENSE REVOKED
739	NO LIC
740	NO SEATBELT‖ MOTOR VEHICLE VIOLATION - NO LICENSE‖ OPERATION OF MOTOR VEH WHILE UNDER INFLUENCE OF‖ FAILURE OF OWNER OR OPERATOR OF MOTOR VEHICLE
741	DRIVE:LIC SUSP/ETC:DUI:SPEC VIOL
742	POSSESS/ETC BURGLARY TOOLS
743	DRIVE W/O LICENSE
744	BATTERY ON PERSON
745	DRIVE:LIC SUSP/ETC:DUI:SPEC VIOL
746	SEE COMMENT FOR CHARGE
	SEE COMMENT FOR CHARGE
747	NO ARREST RECEIVED‖ SEE COMMENT FOR CHARGE
748	DRIVE:LIC SUS/ETC:DUI/RFUSE TST
749	DUI ALCOHOL/0.08 PERCENT
	VIO CRT ORD TO PREVNT DOMESTC VIOL
750	DRIVE:LIC SUSP/ETC:DUI:SPEC VIOL
751	DRIVE:LIC SUSP/ETC:DUI:SPEC VIOL
752	NO ARREST RECEIVED‖ DRIVE W/SUSPENDED LICENSE
753	SEE COMMENT FOR CHARGE
754	BATTERY

ALIEN	CONVICTION(S)
755	DRIVE W/O LICENSE
756	DUI ALCOHOL/0.08 PERCENT
757	VIO CRT ORD TO PREVNT DOMESTC VIOL
	SEE COMMENT FOR CHARGE
758	BATTERY
759	DRIVE W/O LICENSE
760	DUI ALCOHOL/0.08 PERCENT
761	CONTEMPT:VIOL PROTECTIVE ORD/ETC
762	1. HIT AND RUN: PROPERTY DAMAGE; 2. DRIVE: LIC SUS/ETC: DUI/RFUSE TST
763	DRIVE WHILE LIC SUSPEND/ETC
764	DRIVE WHILE LIC SUSPEND/ETC
765	MFG/SALE/ETC LEADED CANE/BILLY/ETC
766	NO ARREST RECEIVED‖ DRIVE W/O LICENSE
767	DUI ALCOHOL/0.08 PERCENT‖ DUI ALCOHOL/DRUGS
768	DUI:ALCOHOL/DRUGS
	DUI ALCOHOL/0.08 PERCENT‖ DUI ALCOHOL/DRUGS
769	NO ARREST RECEIVED‖ SEE COMMENT FOR CHARGE‖ DRIVE WHILE LICENSE SUSP FOR DUI‖ DUI ALCOHOL/DRUGS
770	DRIVE:LIC SUSP/ETC:DUI:SPEC VIOL
771	GRAND THEFT FROM PERSON‖ PROBATION VIOL:REARREST/REVOKE
772	DRIVE WHILE LIC SUSPEND/ETC
773	DRIVE:LIC SUSP/ETC:DUI:SPEC VIOL
774	DUI ALCOHOL/0.08 PERCENT L L BATTERY
775	DISTURBS BY LOUD/UNREASONABLE NOISE
776	DUI ALCOHOL/0.08 PERCENT‖ DRIVE WHILE LIC SUSPEND/ETC
777	UNSAFE SPEED:PREVAILING CONDITIONS
778	DRIVING WHILE INTOXICATED BAC >= 0.15
779	FAIL TO IDENTIFY GIVING FALSE/FICTITIOUS INFO
780	FRAUD-IMPERSON
	LARCENY
781	MOVING TRAFFIC VIOL
782	NONMOVING TRAFFIC VIOL
783	HIT AND RUN‖ NONMOVING TRAFFIC VIOL
784	COCAINE-POSSESS
785	DRUGS - 2ND DEGREE - SALE 3 GRAMS OR MORE -
786	TRAFFIC REGULATION-UNINSURED VEHICLE-OWNER

ALIEN	CONVICTION(S)
787	TRAFFIC - DWI - THIRD-DEGREE DRIVING WHILE
	SECOND-DEGREE DRIVING WHILE IMPAIRED.
788	DRUGS - POSSESSION OF DRUG PARAPHERNALIA - USE OR
	BURGLARY-1ST DEG-ASSAULT PERSON IN BUILD/ON‖ BURGLARY-1ST DEG-POSS DANGEROUS WEAPON/EXPLOSIVE
789	TRAFFIC - DWI - OPERATE MOTOR VEHICLE - ALCOHOL
790	TRAFFIC - DWI - OPERATE MOTOR VEHICLE UNDER
791	TRAFFIC - DWI - OPERATE MOTOR VEHICLE UNDER
792	ASSAULT IN THE FIFTH DEGREE.
793	DUI OF ALCOHOL OR CONTRL SUBST
794	OBSTRUCT/ETC PUBLIC OFFICER/ETC
	FORCE/ADW NOT FIREARM:GBI LIKELY
795	NO ARREST RECEIVED‖ DRIVE W/O LICENSE
796	TRANSPORT/ETC CNTL SUB
797	MOTOR VEHICLE VIOLATION - NO LICENSE
798	NO DRIVERS LICENSE/PERMIT
799	UNLAWFUL TRANSPORT OF FIREARMS - ETC. FELONY‖ PENALTIES FOR FIREARMS FELONY
800	TRAFFIC OFFENSE
801	PERMIT UNLIC GAME ON PREMISES GROSS MISD
802	POSS SCH I, II, III, IV C/S, (1ST/2ND)
803	III/DRUG PARAPHERNALIA-POSSESS/USE,FEL
804	AGGRAVATED DUI
805	SHOPLIFTING-REMOVAL OF GOODS
	DRUG PARAPHERNALIA-POSSESS/USE
806	DUI-LIQUOR/DRUGS/VAPORS/COMBO
807	FORGERY-OFFERS FORGED INSTRUM
	POSS WPN BY PROHIB PERSON
808	EXTREME DUI-BAC .15-.20
809	DANGEROUS DRUG VIOLATION‖ DANGEROUS DRUG-POSS FOR SALE
810	BESTIAL-SEXUAL CONTC ANIMAL
811	EXTREME DUI-BAC .15 OR MORE
812	AGG DUI-LIC SUSP/REV FOR DUI
813	MARIJUANA-POSSESS/USE
814	DRIVE W/LIC SUSP/REVOKE/CANC
815	DUI-LIQUOR/DRUGS/VAPORS/COMBO
816	DUI W/BAC OF .08 OR MORE‖ DUI-LIQUOR/DRUGS/VAPORS/COMBO
817	AGG DUI-LIC SUSP/REV FOR DUI

ALIEN	CONVICTION(S)
818	AGGRAVATED DUI-INTERLOCK
819	8 USC 1325A1 ENTRY WITHOUT INSPECTION, TIME OR PLACE NOT DESIGNATED
820	ENTRY WITHOUT INSPECTION, TIME OR PLACE NOT DESIGNATED
821	ILLEGAL ENTRY
	8 USC 1325 ILLEGAL ENTRY
822	DRIVING WHILE INTOXICATED 2ND
823	LARCENY
824	BATTERY
825	THEFT LESS THAN $100.00
826	VIO CS/DRUG/DEV AND COSMETIC ACT
827	DWI - FOURTH-DEGREE DRIVING WHILE IMPAIRED;
828	NONMOVING TRAFFIC VIOL
829	BATTERY|| DRUGS - EQUIP - POSSESS|| DISORDERLY INTOX
830	NONMOVING TRAFFIC VIOL
831	LARCENY|| MOVING TRAFFIC VIOL
832	NONMOVING TRAFFIC VIOL
833	DUI OF ALCOHOL OR CONTRL SUBST
834	HIT AND RUN:DEATH OR INJURY
835	THEFT
	NO ARREST RECEIVED|| INFL CRPL INJ:SPOUSE/COHAB/DATE
836	COCAINE-POSSESS
837	DRIVING WITHOUT A VALID LICENSE (MISDEMEANOR)
838	DRIVING WITHOUT A VALID LICENSE (MISDEMEANOR)
839	KNOWINGLY DRIVING MOTOR VEHICLE ON SUSPENDED, CANCELED, OR REVOKED REGISTRATION|| DRIVING WITHOUT A VALID LICENSE (MISDEMEANOR)
840	DRIVING WITHOUT A VALID LICENSE (MISDEMEANOR)
841	8 USC 1325 ILLEGAL ENTRY
842	DRIVING WITHOUT A VALID LICENSE (MISDEMEANOR)
843	RECKLESS CONDUCT
844	DRIVING WHILE INTOXICATED 2ND
	ASSAULT CAUSES BODILY INJURY FAMILY MEMBER
845	DRIVING WHILE INTOXICATED 2ND
846	POSSESS CONTROLLED SUBSTANCE
847	NO ARREST RECEIVED|| DRIVE W/O LICENSE
	NO ARREST RECEIVED|| DRIVE W/O LICENSE

ALIEN	CONVICTION(S)
848	POSSESS STOLEN VEHICLE/VESSEL/ETC‖ TAKE VEH W/O OWN CONSENT/VEH THEFT
849	NO ARREST RECEIVED‖ POSSESS UNLAW PARAPHERNALIA‖ FAIL TO APPEAR AFTER WRITTEN PROMISE
	OBSTRUCT/ETC PUBLIC OFFICER/ETC‖ POSSESS/ETC BURGLARY TOOLS
850	BURGLARY‖ USE/UNDER INFL CONTRLD SUBSTANCE‖ RECEIVE/ETC KNOWN STOLEN PROPERTY
851	ASSAULT WITH FIREARM ON PERSON
852	DUI:ALCOHOL/DRUGS
	DUI:ALCOHOL/DRUGS
	DISTURBS BY LOUD/UNREASONABLE NOISE
853	POSSESS CONTROLLED SUBSTANCE
854	THREATEN CRIME WITH INTENT TO TERRORIZE
855	POSSESS STOLLEN VEHICLE/VESSEL/ETC
856	POSSESS CONTROLLED SUBSTANCE
857	INFLICT CORPORAL INJ SPOUSE/COHAB
	RECEIVE/ETC KNOWN STOLEN PROPERTY‖ CONTEMPT:DISOBEY COURT ORDER/ETC
858	DUI ALCOHOL/DRUGS
859	GAMBLING
860	POSSESS CONTROLLED SUBSTANCE
861	ROBBERY
862	NO ARREST RECEIVED‖ INFRACTION VIOLATION
	POSSESS CONTROLLED SUBSTANCE‖ POSSESS CONTROL SUBSTANCE PARAPHERNA
	VANDALISM
863	DUI ALCOHOL/DRUGS
864	POSSESS CONTROLLED SUBSTANCE‖ POSS MARIJUANA 28.5- GRAMS
865	NO ARREST RECEIVED‖ DRIVE W/O LICENSE
866	THEFT‖ FAIL TO APPEAR AFTER WRITTEN PROMISE
867	DISORDERLY CONDUCT:INTOX DRUG/ALCOH
868	BURGLARY
	NO ARREST RECEIVED‖ THEFT
869	NO ARREST RECEIVED‖ DRIVE W/O LICENSE
870	DRIVE W/O LICENSE
871	POSSESS NARC CONTROL SUBSTANCE
872	DUI ALCOHOL/0.08 PERCENT
873	THREATEN CRIME W/INTENT TO TERRORIZE

ALIEN	CONVICTION(S)
874	DUI ALCOHOL/0.08 PERCENT
875	CONTEMPT:DISOBEY COURT ORDER/ETC
876	DRIVE W/O LICENSE
877	DRIVE:LIC SUSP/ETC:DUI:SPEC VIOL
878	DRIVE:LIC SUSP/ETC:DUI:SPEC VIOL
879	CONVICTION OCCURRED ON 11/26/2013 FOR INFLICT CORPORAL INJ SPOUSE/COHAB
880	BURGLARY‖ STOLEN PROP-DEAL IN
881	CHRG 14601,5 (VC)
882	CHRG242-243(E)(1) PC
883	DUI ALCOHOL/0.08 PERCENT
	DRIVE:LIC SUSP/ETC:DUI:SPEC VIOL‖ DUI ALCOHOL/DRUGS
	DRIVE: LIC SUSP/ETC:DUI:SPEC VIOL
884	POSSESS CONTROLLED SUBSTANCE
	NO ARREST RECEIVED‖ POSSESS CONTROL SUBSTANCE PARAPHERNA
	POSSESS CONTROLLED SUBSTANCE
	POSSESS CONTROLLED SUBSTANCE
885	POSSESS CONTROLLED SUBSTANCE
	POSSESS CONTROL SUBSTANCE PARAPHERNA
886	POSSESS NARC CONTROL SUBSTANCE
887	BURGLARY
888	DRIVING W/O LICENSE
	DRIVING W/O LICENSE
889	DRIVE W/O LICENSE
890	CHRG 23152 (B) - 23550 VC
891	POSSESS CONTROLLED SUBSTANCE‖ BURGLARY:SECOND DEGREE
892	CONTEMPT:VIOL PROTECTIVE ORD/ETC
893	DRIVE W/O LICENSE
894	CHRG 242-243€ (1) PC
895	DUI ALCOHOL/0.08 PERCENT AND DRIVE: LIC SUS/ETC:DUI RFUSE TST
896	FALSE ID TO SPECIFIC PEACE OFICERS
897	DUI ALCOHOL/0.08 PERCENT‖ DRIVE:LIC SUSP/ETC:DUI:SPEC VIOL
898	TAMPER WITH VEHICLE
899	PETTY THEFT W/PR JAIL:SPEC OFFENSES
900	DLR/ETC UNDETRIME OWNER:STLN PROP
901	NO ARREST RECEIVED‖ DRIVE W/O LICENSE
902	POSSESS CONTROLLED SUBSTANCE
903	DISORDERLY CONDUCT:INTOX DRUG/ALCOH

ALIEN	CONVICTION(S)
904	BATTERY: SPOUSE/EX SP/DATE/ETC
905	NO ARREST RECEIVED‖ VANDALISM
	CARJACKING‖ THREATEN CRIME WITH INTENT TO TERRORIZE
906	NO ARREST RECEIVED‖ SEX OFFENDER FAIL REG/ETC
907	POSSESS CONTROLLED SUBSTANCE
908	RECEIVE/ETC KNOWN STOLEN PROPERTY
909	POSSESS CONTROL SUBSTANCE FOR SALE
910	POSSESS CONTROLLED SUBSTANCE
911	FORGE OFFICIAL SEAL‖ POSSESS CNTL SUBSTANCE
912	ENTER/ETC NONCOMMERCIAL DWELLING
913	DUI ALCOHOL/0.08 PERCENT
914	DUI ALCOHOL/0.08 PERCENT AND DRIVE:LIC SUSP/ETC: SPEC VIOL
915	UNLAWFUL USE/ETC:DRIVER LIC
916	INFLICT CORPORAL INJ SPOUSE/COHAB
917	NO ARREST RECEIVED‖ DRIVE:LIC SUSP/ETC:DUI:SPEC VIOL
918	POSSESS CONTROLLED SUBSTANCE‖ MFG/SALE/ETC LEADED CANE/BILLY/ETC
919	DUI ALCOHOL/0.08 PERCENT AND DRIVE:LIC SUSP/ETC: SPEC VIOL
920	L&L ACTS W/CHILD:AGE SPECIFIC
921	NO ARREST RECEIVED‖ OWNER ALLOW UNLICENSED OPR VEHICLE
922	DUI ALCOHOL/DRUGS CAUSE BODILY INJ
923	POSS CS PG 3< 28G
924	USE/UNDER INFL CONTRLD SUBSTANCE
	PETTY THEFT
	NO ARREST RECEIVED‖ SEE COMMENT FOR CHARGE
925	TAKE VEH W/O OWN CONSENT/VEH THEFT
926	NO ARREST RECEIVED‖ SEE COMMENT FOR CHARGE
927	OBSTURCT/ETC PUBLIC OFFICER/ETC
928	DUI ALCOHOL
929	CARRY CONCEALED DIRK OR DAGGER
930	POSSESS CONTROLLED SUBSTANCE AND MFG/ETC DECEPT GOVT ID/DRVIE LIC
931	MAKE/PASS FICTITIOUS CHECK
932	DRIVE W/O LICENSE
933	POSSESS CONTROLLED SUBSTANCE‖ TRANSPORT/ETC CNTL SUB‖ DRIVE:SUSPENDED/ETC LIC:RECKLESS
934	INFLICT CORPORAL INJ SPOUSE/COHAB

ALIEN	CONVICTION(S)
935	DRIVING WITH SUSPENDED/REVOKED DRIVER'S LICENSE|| FAILURE OF OWNER OR OPERATOR OF MOTOR VEHICLE|| NO SEATBELT
936	DRIVING WITHOUT A VALID LICENSE (MISDEMEANOR)
937	DRIVING WITHOUT A VALID LICENSE (MISDEMEANOR)
938	DRIVING WITHOUT A VALID LICENSE (MISDEMEANOR)
939	DRIVING WITHOUT A VALID LICENSE (MISDEMEANOR)
940	NONMOVING TRAFFIC VIOL
941	HARASSMENT
	CRIMINAL MISCHIEF
942	DISORDERLY CONDUCT
943	8 USC 1325 ILLEGAL ENTRY (M)
944	ACCIDENT INV DEATH/PERS INJURY
945	DRIVING WHILE INTOXICATED
946	DWI - LEVEL 4
947	DRIVING WHILE INTOXICATED 2ND
948	DRIVING WHILE LICENSE SUSPENDED OR REVOKED (MISDEMEANOR)
949	CONTRIBUTING DEL OF JUVENILE
950	DISORDERLY CONDUCT
951	BURGLARY|| POSSESS CNTL SUBSTANCE
952	BURGLARY:SECOND DEGREE
	POSSESS NARC CONTROL SUBSTANCE
953	DUI ALCOHOL/0.08 PERCENT|| DRIVE:LIC SUSP/ETC:DUI:SPEC VIOL
954	NO ARREST RECEIVED|| DRIVE W/O LICENSE
955	DUI ALCOHOL/0.08 PERCENT
956	DRIVE W/SUSPENDED LICENSE
957	BURGLARY
958	DUI ALCOHOL/DRUGS
959	USE/UNDER INFLUENCE CONTROL SUBST
960	INFLICT CORPORAL INJ SPOUSE/COHAB|| CHILD CRUELTY:POS INJURY/DEATH|| PROBATION VIOL:REARREST/REVOKE|| DRIVE W/O LICENSE|| UNSAFE SPEED:PREVAILING CONDITIONS|| FAIL PROVE FIN RSP:PO REQUEST|| FAIL TO APPEAR:WRITTEN PROMISE|| LOCAL ORDINANCE VIOLATION
961	POSSESS CONTROLLED SUBSTANCE|| FALSE ID TO SPECIFIC PEACE OFICERS|| DISORDERLY CONDUCT:INTOX DRUG/ALCOH|| BURGLARY:SECOND DEGREE
	POSSESS CONTROLLED SUBSTANCE|| BURGLARY:SECOND DEGREE
962	DUI:ALCOHOL/DRUGS

ALIEN	CONVICTION(S)
963	URINATING IN PUBLIC
964	DISP / NO COMPLAINT FIELD
965	SHOPLIFTING-REMOVAL OF GOODS
966	FAIL TO NOTIFY/STRIKE FIXTURE
967	DISP / NO COMPLAINT FIELD
968	FAIL TO SHOW DRIV LIC OR ID
969	DUI-LIQUOR/DRUGS/VAPORS/COMBO
970	VIOLATION OF PROMISE TO APPEAR
971	CRIMINAL TRESPASS 2ND DEG
972	DISPO/ COURT DISMISSAL
973	AGG DUI-LIC SUSP/REV FOR DUI
974	AGGRAVATED ASSAULT‖ DANGEROUS DRUG-POSS/USE
975	METH-MFG PHYS INJURY LT 15 YR
976	MARIJUANA-POSSESS/USE
977	INDECENT EXPOSURE
978	DRIVE W/LIC SUSP/REVOKE/CANC
979	ASSAULT-INTENT/RECKLESS/INJURE
980	TRAFFIC REGULATION - CRIMINAL PENALTY FOR FAILURE
981	TRAFFIC REGULATION - DRIVER MUST CARRY PROOF OF
982	DRIVING WHILE INTOXICATED 2ND
983	DRIVING WHILE INTOXICATED BAC >= 0.15
984	DISTURB PEACE
985	NARCOTIC DRUG-POSSESS/USE
986	CARRY DEADLY WPN < 21 YOA
987	DRIVE UNDER INFLUENCE:-21‖ DRIVE WHILE LIC SUSPEND/ETC
988	DUI:ALCOHOL/DRUGS
989	POSSESS CONTROLLED SUBSTANCE
990	DUI ALCOHOL/DRUGS
991	LEWD OR LASCIV ACTS W/CHILD UNDER 14
992	FORCE/ADW NOT FIREARM:GBI LIKELY
993	DUI ALCOHOL/0.08 PERCENT
994	CONTEMPT:CRT:DISORD/ETC BEHAVIOR
995	DUI ALCOHOL/0.08 PERCENT
996	DRIVING WITHOUT A VALID LICENSE (MISDEMEANOR)
997	BAT:SPOUSE/EX SP/DATE/ETC
998	FALSE ID TO SPECIFIC PEACE OFICERS
999	VIO CRT ORD TO PREVNT DOMESTC VIOL

ALIEN	CONVICTION(S)
1000	DOMESTIC ABUSE ACT.

Notes:

[1]Convictions are taken directly from the rap sheet located in the Federal Bureau of Investigation's National Crime Information Center (NCIC). As a result, some convictions may contain entries such as "No Arrest Received" or "See Comment For Charge." Additional detail about the related crime(s) for these cases may be found either in local systems or courthouses.